CALUMET CITY PUBLIC LIBRARY

SO-AQL-576

3 1613 00435 6393

J B PER

PER

JPER 26.00 5-13

BLUE BANNER BIOGRAPHY

KATY PERRY

Michelle Medlock Adams

Mitchell Lane
PUBLISHERS

P.O. Box 196
Hockessin, Delaware 19707
Visit us on the web: www.mitchelllane.com
Comments? email us: mitchelllane@mitchelllane.com

CALUMET CITY PUBLIC
LIBRARY

Mitchell Lane
PUBLISHERS

Copyright © 2012 by Mitchell Lane Publishers. All rights reserved. No part of this book may be reproduced without written permission from the publisher. Printed and bound in the United States of America.

Printing   1   2   3   4   5   6   7   8   9

Blue Banner Biographies

Alicia Keys	Gwen Stefani	Megan Fox
Allen Iverson	Ice Cube	Miguel Tejada
Ashanti	Ja Rule	Nancy Pelosi
Ashlee Simpson	Jamie Foxx	Natasha Bedingfield
Ashton Kutcher	Jay-Z	Orianthi
Avril Lavigne	Jennifer Lopez	Orlando Bloom
Beyoncé	Jessica Simpson	P. Diddy
Blake Lively	J. K. Rowling	Peyton Manning
Bow Wow	Joe Flacco	Pink
Brett Favre	John Legend	Prince William
Britney Spears	Justin Berfield	Queen Latifah
CC Sabathia	Justin Timberlake	Rihanna
Carrie Underwood	Kanye West	Robert Downey Jr.
Chris Brown	Kate Hudson	Robert Pattinson
Chris Daughtry	**Katy Perry**	Ron Howard
Christina Aguilera	Keith Urban	Sean Kingston
Ciara	Kelly Clarkson	Selena
Clay Aiken	Kenny Chesney	Shakira
Cole Hamels	Ke$ha	Shia LaBeouf
Condoleezza Rice	Kristen Stewart	Shontelle Layne
Corbin Bleu	Lady Gaga	Soulja Boy Tell 'Em
Daniel Radcliffe	Lance Armstrong	Stephenie Meyer
David Ortiz	Leona Lewis	Taylor Swift
David Wright	Lil Wayne	T.I.
Derek Jeter	Lindsay Lohan	Timbaland
Drew Brees	Ludacris	Tim McGraw
Eminem	Mariah Carey	Toby Keith
Eve	Mario	Usher
Fergie	Mary J. Blige	Vanessa Anne Hudgens
Flo Rida	Mary-Kate and Ashley Olsen	Zac Efron

Library of Congress Cataloging-in-Publication Data
Adams, Michelle Medlock.
 Katy Perry / by Michelle Medlock Adams.
    p. cm. — (Blue banner biographies)
Includes bibliographical references and index.
ISBN 978-1-61228-051-6 (library bound)
1. Perry, Katy—Juvenile literature. 2. Singers—United States—Biography—Juvenile literature.
I. Title.
ML3930.P455A63 2012
782.42164092—dc22
[B]
                                                                                          2011016774
eBook ISBN: 9781612281780

ABOUT THE AUTHOR: Michelle Medlock Adams graduated with a journalism degree from Indiana University. She has written 44 books and thousands of articles for newspapers, web sites, and magazines. She resides in Indiana with her husband, Jeff, and their daughters, Abby and Ally. To find out more about Michelle, visit her web site at http://www.michellemedlockadams.com.

PUBLISHER'S NOTE: The following story has been thoroughly researched, and to the best of our knowledge represents a true story. While every possible effort has been made to ensure accuracy, the publisher will not assume liability for damages caused by inaccuracies in the data and makes no warranty on the accuracy of the information contained herein. This story has not been authorized or endorsed by Katy Perry.

Blue Banner Biography

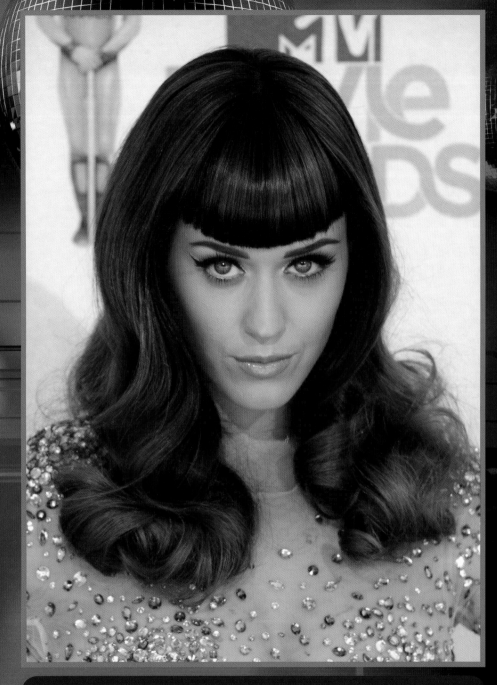

Never one to be shy, Katy Perry gives new meaning to the phrase "true blue" with this look. Ironically, Katy is the voice of a blue Smurfette in the 2011 movie **The Smurfs**.

A Rebel With a Cause

Superstar Katy Perry could have had her pick of dates for the 2011 Grammy Awards Show, but she chose to take her 90-year-old grandmother Anne as her companion. Together, the twosome walked the Red Carpet, drawing the attention of reporters and photographers. Katy wore large white angel wings, and Anne stole the show with a blinged-out cane.

Just then, a reporter with *Access Hollywood* stopped Anne and asked her which of Katy's songs was her favorite one. Obviously offering a bit of help, Katy whispered something to her grandma. Immediately, Anne fired back, "Oh yes, 'I Kissed a Girl' because it made her famous."

Following up, the reporter asked, "What did you think about that song when it first came out?"

"Yeah, what did you think of it, Grandma?" Katy chimed in.

"Well, I thought it was terrible," admitted Grandma Anne, chuckling.

Laughing with her honest grandma, Katy added, "This is the type of relationship we have . . . she just tells me to take out the trash."

Though Katy didn't win any Grammys that evening, she was honored to have received seven nominations.

The middle child of two pastors, Katheryn "Katy" Hudson grew up with lots of love and lots of rules. Her parents, Keith and Mary Hudson, were pastors of a non-denominational Christian church, and they allowed only Christian music in their house. Katy grew up singing in her church and never hearing Madonna, Cher, Pat Benatar, Cyndi Lauper, or any other secular music artists. She missed out on watching music videos, too, because MTV and VH1 were permanently blocked on all the TVs in her house.

> *Every beat, every vocal, every guitar solo thrilled Katy to the core, and she wanted more Queen, more rock, more music.*

That didn't keep Katy from dreaming about secular music and the famous music-makers of the day. The rebel rocker inside her was longing to get out. Then one day, it happened. One of Katy's good friends at school—a really popular girl—invited Katy to her house for a slumber party. While at that party, Katy heard "Killer Queen" by Queen, and she fell in love with the band's lead singer, Freddie Mercury.

It was life-changing for Katy, who had heard only gospel music up to that point in her life. Every beat, every vocal, every guitar solo thrilled her to the core, and she wanted more Queen, more rock, more music.

From that moment on, nine-year-old Katy was definitely hooked on music—especially rock—and begged her parents to let her tag along with her older sister when she went to her

Katy's parents, Mary and Keith Hudson, have always been supportive of their daughter's career.

singing lessons. At age 13, Katy decided she wanted to do more than sing. She wanted to play guitar, too. She picked out a beautiful royal blue guitar and began practicing many hours. Two years later, she was regularly making trips from her hometown in Santa Barbara, California, to Nashville, Tennessee, in order to meet the movers and shakers in the Christian music industry. Her strong vocals and passionate guitar playing gained the attention of several important people.

"That's when I started recording and meeting people and learned how to write a song, craft it, and play my guitar better," Katy said in an interview with journalist Leah Greenblatt on *EW.com*. "My parents had some connections in the gospel industry. It was like my school of rock."

But like most school experiences, Katy didn't ace every test. In 2001, at age 17, Katy released her gospel album, simply titled *Katy Hudson*. Her debut release wasn't exactly successful.

"It reached literally maybe 100 people," Katy told *EW.com*, "and then the label went bankrupt. It was not like I was Amy Grant or something. So I went back home."

Still, Katy showed promise. In fact, Russ Breimeier of *Christianity Today* gave her debut album a favorable review, calling her "a remarkable young talent emerging, a gifted songwriter in her own right who will almost certainly go far in this business."

Mr. Breimeier spoke the truth. Little did Katy know that just seven years later, she would be voted Best New Artist of 2008 by the readers of *Rolling Stone*. But those seven years in between would be paved with broken promises and disappointments. She would have to believe in herself to make it in the competitive music business, drawing on the faith her parents had instilled in her as a child.

> "That's when I started recording and meeting people and learned how to write a song, craft it, and play my guitar better."

Katy Perry Hudson: The Early Years

On October 25, 1984, Katheryn Elizabeth Hudson came into this world, blessing her parents Keith and Mary Hudson and big sister, Angela, of Santa Barbara, California. Later, David Hudson came along and completed the happy Hudson family. The Hudsons were very religious. In fact, Katy's parents were and still are Evangelical pastors. The church has played a very important role in Katy's life, while giving her the opportunity to sing in public.

"My dad would give me ten dollars, which is a lot of money when you're nine, to sing at church, on tables at restaurants, at family functions, just about anywhere," Katy shared on *Lyricsreg.com*. Katy and Angela both took singing lessons. In fact, Katy enrolled at the Music Academy of the West in Santa Barbara and studied Italian opera for a short time. Later she learned how to play the guitar. (She still plays—both acoustic and electric.) But Katy was growing bored with gospel music.

"The only things I was allowed to listen to were the *Sister Act 1* and 2 soundtracks," Katy told *Entertainment Weekly*. These comedies feature Catholic nuns.

By the time she turned 13, she was no longer satisfied to sit in the pews at church. She took swing dancing lessons and fell even more in love with music and performing.

"I started swing dancing, [doing the] lindy hop and jitterbug," Katy explained in the book *Russell Brand & Katy Perry – The Love Story*, by David Stone. "I would go to the Santa Barbara rec hall and I would learn how to dance there. I was taught by some of the more seasoned dancers."

> "I was always the kid at the dinner table who, if there was a line you shouldn't cross, I took a big leap over it."

Katy could see herself performing and dancing and singing the songs she had written on a stage somewhere other than in a church. While she respected her parents and their rules, she couldn't help wanting more. She began rebelling a bit against her strict Christian household, even piercing her nose.

"I have, I guess, pushed [my parents'] envelope from the day I was born," shared Katy on *Beliefnet.com*. "I was always the kid at the dinner table who, if there was a line you shouldn't cross, I took a big leap over it. That's always been me. There's never really been, like, an edit button on my keyboard of life."

Katy knew in her heart that it was time to pursue her music career full out, and there was no way she could do that and regularly attend Dos Pueblos High School in Santa Barbara. She earned her GED after her freshman year and began working on her unsuccessful gospel album in Nashville. She learned some things about her music, the music industry, and herself during that time in Nashville.

"When I started out in gospel music, my perspective then was a bit enclosed and very strict. Everything I had in my life at that time was very church-related," Katy said in Stone's book. "I didn't know there was another world that existed beyond that. So when I left home and saw all of that, it was like, 'Omigosh, I fell down the rabbit hole and there's this whole Alice in Wonderland right there!' My motto from then on was to live life to the fullest, because at the end you're dead."

When Katy came home to Santa Barbara, the teen was more determined than ever to make it in the music industry, despite her first failed gospel album. She continued growing, writing, playing, learning, singing, and recording. She changed her name from Katy Hudson to Katy Perry—Perry was her mother's maiden name. Her reason? She felt that Katy Hudson sounded too much like the name of the famous actress Kate Hudson, and she wanted to avoid that confusion. Katy took some time to reinvent herself, and then she headed to Los Angeles.

> "My motto from then on was to live life to the fullest, because at the end you're dead."

Katy wows the New York Z100 listening audience with her singing and guitar playing in 2008. Though she's known for her strong vocals and striking beauty, Katy can play both the acoustic and electric guitar with great skill.

A Bumpy Road

*S*ome Hollywood success stories are paved with big breaks and powerful connections. Katy's was not. She encountered many bumps on her road to success, but she just kept going because she truly believed she would someday make it in the music industry.

When she arrived in Los Angeles at age 17, she was thankful to get the opportunity to work with a talented man named Glen Ballard. Katy learned that Ballard had produced Alanis Morissette's super successful album *Jagged Little Pill*, as well as writing and producing hit records for Michael Jackson and Wilson Phillips, to name a few.

"I came from Santa Barbara to Los Angeles with a wonderful producer named Glen Ballard, who brought me out here and kinda looked out for me for three years," Katy told MTV. Some days, she would write her rent check and pray that God would help the check clear. Times were tough financially and emotionally; still, she pressed on.

In 2003—the year she turned 19—Katy signed a record deal with Island Def Jam. It looked as if her dreams were finally coming true. In addition, her talent started drawing attention. The Matrix (Scott Spock, Lauren Christy, and Graham Edwards), who wrote and produced hits for superstars Avril Lavigne, Shakira, Britney Spears, and Hilary Duff, took notice of Katy and asked her to be one of two vocalists on their debut album. By 2004, Katy had two albums in the works—her solo record with Glen Ballard and the one with The Matrix. To top it all off, the October 2004 issue of *Blender* called Katy "The Next Big Thing."

Katy worked with Lauren Christy (left) of The Matrix. Her album with that famous group never saw the light of day. The project was shelved, but Katy went on to find fame of her own.

Katy could hardly wait for the first single, "Broken," to debut from The Matrix album. They had already shot the video for that song, and Katy was in it, wearing a 1950s-inspired outfit with fun high heels.

To her disappointment, people never got the chance to see her retro outfit in the video or buy the song, because The Matrix put the whole album on hold indefinitely. Katy focused all her effort on her other album and dreamed about the day she would perform her songs live. Then, as time grew closer for its release, disappointment struck again. Island Def Jam dropped her. She couldn't believe it.

Katy continued working and eventually signed with Columbia Records. She cowrote 11 songs for that album and shot videos for several of the top tracks. In fact, one of those songs, "Simple," ended up on the sound track for the movie *The Sisterhood of the Traveling Pants*. It wasn't enough. Columbia decided not to release her album after all.

Ballard stood by her through all the letdowns. "Nobody at those labels got what she was about," he said in Stone's book. "She had talent, personality, humor, a sense of fashion. They didn't know what to do with it."

Jason Flom, who was the CEO of Capitol Music at the time, knew exactly what to do with Katy—sign her and finally release her music for everyone to experience. He signed her in the spring of 2007, and she began working with Dr. Luke and Max Martin. They helped her crank out her breakout hit, "I Kissed a Girl." That catchy song went on to top the Billboard Hot 100 for seven straight weeks, making Katy Perry a household name. That same year, she also offered a free download of her song "Ur So Gay," which was also an instant hit.

It had been a long road to that first breakout hit, but Katy was well on her way to being taken seriously as a songwriter, a musician, and a performer.

Known for her eclectic style and flashy outfits, Katy loves to surprise her fans with multicolored hair, fun accessories, and retro looks.

Open Doors

Katy's music was fun, upbeat, and great for dancing, and it was grabbing the attention of superstars such as Madonna, who actually mentioned her on KISS FM and KRQ's *Johnjay and Rich* morning show in Arizona. Doors began opening for Katy. For example, on March 10, 2008, she appeared as herself on the ABC Family television series *Wildfire* in an episode titled, "Life's Too Short." That summer she appeared as herself on the daytime soap opera *The Young and the Restless*.

After a two-month tour of radio stations promoting "I Kissed a Girl," Katy joined the 2008 Warped Tour music festival, which proved to be a smart move in establishing her fan base. She didn't want to be thought of as a one-hit wonder, and she didn't want to be seen as a pretty pop princess. She wanted the world to know that she was a rocker, a woman who wrote all her own music, a serious musician.

The infamous Warped Tour crowds are made up of die-hard rockers and fans of alternative bands like Chiodos and Gym Class Heroes, and Katy hoped they would embrace her, too. She had already appeared in a music video for Gym

CALUMET CITY PUBLIC LIBRARY

Class Heroes' "Cupid's Chokehold," playing the girlfriend of lead singer Travis McCoy. That role turned into real life for Katy, who started seriously dating McCoy. Concert after concert, she bounded onstage wearing denim shorts with the letters *KP* in hot pink glitter plastered across her back pockets, dancing with a giant tube of lip balm. She rocked out, but she did it the Katy way, and the fans loved her. McCoy loved her, too, and even gave her a promise ring, but their romance was on-again, off-again all year.

> *Concert after concert, she bounded onstage with the letters KP in hot pink glitter plastered across her back pockets.*

That same summer, her album *One of the Boys* debuted and peaked at #9 on Hot 100, and "I Kissed a Girl" earned her a Grammy nomination for Best Female Pop Vocal Performance. In addition, she was nominated in five categories at the 2008 MTV Video Music Awards, including Best New Artist and Best Female Video, but she lost to pop diva Britney Spears. However, the awards season wasn't over. Katy won Best New Act at the 2008 MTV Europe Music Awards, which she also co-hosted, and Best International Female Solo Artist at the 2009 BRIT Awards. Just when she thought it couldn't get any better, both "I Kissed a Girl" and "Hot n Cold" were certified three-time platinum by the Recording Industry Association of America for individual digital sales of more than 3 million copies.

While her career was blossoming, her love life was not. She and McCoy tried to rekindle their romance in April 2009 but eventually broke it off for good. Luckily, Katy was too busy to be sad for long. She recorded songs with other superstars and even taped her own acoustic special on MTV, which resulted in another album, *Katy Perry: MTV Unplugged*. All at once, it seemed as if Katy were everywhere — on magazine covers, award shows, talk shows, concert tours, TV specials, and makeup advertisements. Her style was outrageous and funny at times, and classy and vintage too. Just like her music, she kept changing it up and keeping it real.

"I think people can appreciate a songwriter who shows different sides. Everything I write has a sense of humor to it."

"I think people can appreciate a songwriter who shows different sides," Katy shared in an interview. "The whole angst thing is cool, but if that's all you've got, it's just boring. Everything I write, whether it's happy or sad, has a sense of humor to it. Someone told me the other day that I'm a bit like [famous funny lady] Lucille Ball. They said, 'You look pretty put together on the outside, but inside there's just something a bit wrong.' "

As it turns out, two wrongs can make a right.

When Katy met British comedian Russell Brand in 2009, there was an instant connection. Brand, who had starred in *Forgetting Sarah Marshall* and *Bedtime Stories* and would soon appear in the 2010 release of *Get Him to the Greek*, had resurrected his acting career and become a star in his own right. He and Katy had both overcome major obstacles to make it in the difficult world of show business, and neither had given up. Soon, tabloids started reporting that Katy was in a relationship with Brand, and she wasn't denying it.

Katy gets her slime on at the 2010 Nickelodeon Kids' Choice Awards. She was in good company—Justin Bieber also got slimed that day.

Year of the Kitten

*T*hough talented, Brand wasn't exactly the type of guy that a girl would want to introduce to her parents—especially if those parents were pastors. Brand was known as a foul-mouthed comic, a former drug addict and a recovering alcoholic who was rarely politically correct. However, Katy had fallen hard for the bad boy after connecting with him at the 2009 MTV Video Music Awards in New York. Brand was again the host of that event and Katy thought he was funny and very likable. Following the show, they took a secret vacation to Thailand, where their love took root and began to grow. From there, they dated only each other, bouncing between London and L.A.

After several weeks of serious dating, it was time to meet the parents. Keith Hudson gave Brand a copy of his book, *The Cry*, which is a Christian book about finding God. Brand returned the favor by giving him a copy of his autobiography, *My Booky Wook*, which is definitely *not* Christian. Brand goes into great detail about his drug addictions and bad relationships in his book, but Keith and Mary Hudson both enjoyed reading it. Katy's mom told a

After a whirlwind romance, Katy married the love of her life, Russell Brand, in October 2010. "[Russell] never lied to me once. I trust him; there's just a level of trust that we've built up," Katy said of her husband.

British newspaper she could tell that Brand was really hungry for positive influences in his life. "[Katy and Russell] are basically seeking the truth from God—and they are going to find it," she said.

Katy's dad added, "Russell's really got a hunger for the supernatural. He really likes us because he has a whole new, different concept on Christianity now that he has met us."

With "the meeting of Katy's parents" behind them, the couple moved forward in their relationship. After dating only a little more than three months, Brand took Katy on a December trip to India, where he asked her to marry him. He had planned the proposal down to the very last detail, scheduling a spiritual guru to bless the couple, an elephant ride, a fireworks show, and a big engagement ring. Brand had originally planned to ask her to marry him while atop the elephant's back, but the fireworks spooked the animal and they were forced to climb down. Still, with fireworks going off both in the night sky and in Katy's heart, she said yes. She returned to the United States an engaged twenty-five-year-old, ready to plan her wedding.

In the midst of making October 2010 wedding plans, Katy also had some promotional work to do. After all, her follow-up album to *One of the Boys* was scheduled for an August release, and she was determined to make it better than anything she had ever done before.

Mission accomplished. *Teenage Dream* debuted at #1 on Billboard's Top 200 Albums Chart, scanning 192,222 units in its first week of release. It made Katy one of the top 10 artists with the bestselling debuts of the year, one of only two pop artists to appear on that list.

The first hit single from *Teenage Dream*—and probably the most talked about summer song of 2010—was "California Gurls," which featured Snoop Dogg. *Entertainment Weekly* called the song "unforgettable." Apparently, many agreed with that statement because "California Gurls" made the quickest climb to #1 since Gwen Stefani's "Hollaback Girl" in the summer of 2005.

"Katy has set records and turned radio upside down," said Greg Thompson, Executive Vice-President for Promotion at Capitol Records, in a press release. "This track has broken all-time spins records, and achieved massive Hot 100 audience numbers of historic proportion."

Performing with Snoop Dogg, Katy Perry belts out her blockbuster hit "California Gurls," which was the summertime theme song of 2010.

That single isn't the only hit on the album. "Teenage Dream," the title track, also made Top 10 lists all over the world, and then "Firework" flooded the airwaves and moved up the charts. "Firework" also became an anthem for those who had been bullied or ever felt they didn't fit in. That made Katy happier than all the awards and critical acclaim she'd enjoyed that year.

"I'm really a people person," she shared in an interview on the *CBS Early Show*. "And I believe in people, and I believe in their good and I believe in their gifts, and I believe that everyone has a talent or a spark."

That's what inspired her to write the song in the first place. She knew the video had to be authentic and powerful, so she didn't hire actors. Instead, the characters in the video are real-life individuals who want to make a difference and give victims a voice. At the end of the "Firework" video, Katy dances with about 250 people, actual fans of the singer. It made for a very impactful performance.

Truly, 2010 turned out to be the Year of the Kitten (Kitten is a nickname of Katy's). She released her own perfume, called Purr. She married the love of her life on October 23 in a traditional Hindu ceremony in India. She had yet another hit album, *Teenage Dream*, and she rocked the runway of the Victoria's Secret Fashion Show, which aired on December 1 on CBS.

Katy and her "Purrfectly" beautiful spokesmodels help launch Katy's signature scent, called Purr. It is the star's first perfume.

With a record 175 million pop-culture fans voting, Katy Perry took home two People's Choice Awards in 2011 for Favorite Online Sensation and Favorite Female Artist.

Katy definitely has a big heart, and she gives big when it comes to charitable causes. Whether it means putting on a special concert to support U.S. troops, designing a T-shirt to be sold as part of H&M's Fashion Against AIDS collection, or playing a round of celebrity *Who Wants to Be a Millionaire?* for St. Jude Children's Research Hospital, she loves to help. She has also supported Generosity Water, Keep-A-Breast, Music for Relief, and Project Clean Water.

Also in December, Katy learned that she had been nominated for four Grammys: Best Female Pop Vocal Performance for "Teenage Dream"; Best Pop Collaboration with Vocals for "California Gurls" with Snoop Dogg; Best Pop Vocal Album for *Teenage Dream*; and Album of the Year for *Teenage Dream*. Though Katy didn't bring home a Grammy in 2011, her performances at the famous awards show received rave reviews. While sitting in a swing and singing "Not Like the Movies," images of her and Brand's wedding showed on the large screen behind her. It seemed quite fitting since the Grammys were held the day before Valentine's Day.

> **Katy Perry has proven she is a star, and she's planning to shine brightly for many years to come.**

"Grammys are like catching shooting stars," Katy told CBS reporter Maggie Rodriguez, "so hopefully one day I'll catch one."

Whether she does or not, Katy Perry has proven she is a star, and she's planning to shine brightly for many years to come.

1984   Katheryn Elizabeth Hudson is born on October 25 in Santa Barbara, California.

1999   Katy drops out of Dos Pueblos High School in Santa Barbara and earns her GED so that she can pursue a music career.

2000   She moves back to Santa Barbara and changes her name from Katy Hudson to Katy Perry.

2001   Her gospel album, *Katy Hudson*, bombs. Katy moves to L.A. to work with producer Glen Ballard.

2003   Katy signs a record deal with Island Def Jam. She signs a record deal with The Matrix to sing on their debut album.

2004   Katy is called "The Next Big Thing" in the October issue of *Blender*. Island Def Jam drops her. The Matrix shelves the album featuring Katy. Katy signs with Columbia Records.

2005   Katy's song "Simple" is released on the sound track of the film *The Sisterhood of the Traveling Pants*. Columbia Records drops her.

2007   Katy signs a record deal with Capitol Music. She releases a free download of her song "Ur So Gay." The digital release of "I Kissed a Girl" goes viral.

2008   Katy appears as herself in the ABC Family series *Wildfire* on March 10. She starts dating Travis McCoy, the lead singer of Gym Class Heroes. Katy appears as herself on *The Young and the Restless* in June. She begins touring as part of the 2008 Warped Tour music festival. Her album, *One of the Boys*, debuts. "I Kissed a Girl" earns a Grammy nomination for Best Female Pop Vocal Performance.

2009   She tapes an acoustic special on MTV, which is released as another album, *Katy Perry: MTV Unplugged*. Katy and McCoy break up for good. Katy connects with Russell Brand at the MTV Video Music Awards, and he proposes to her in India on New Year's Eve.

2010   Katy's album *Teenage Dream* is released in August. She marries Russell Brand on October 23. She performs at The

Victoria Secret's Fashion Show and on VH1 Divas Salute the Troops. She is nominated for four Grammy Awards.

2011   Katy kicks off her California Dreams tour. She appears on MTV's *America's Best Dance Crew* and the hit show *American Idol*. She is featured on the cover of *Vanity Fair*.

DISCOGRAPHY

Singles

2010   "If We Ever Meet Again" (Timbaland featuring Katy Perry)
        "California Gurls" (featuring Snoop Dogg)
        "Teenage Dream"
        "Firework"

2009   "Thinking of You"
        "Waking Up in Vegas"

2008   "Hot n Cold"

2007   "I Kissed a Girl"
        "Ur So Gay" (released as a CD promo single in the U.S.)

Music Videos

2010   "If We Ever Meet Again"
        "California Gurls"
        "Teenage Dream"
        "Firework"

2009   "Thinking of You"
        "Waking Up in Vegas"
        "Starstrukk"

2008   "I Kissed a Girl"
        "Hot n Cold"

2007   "Ur So Gay"

Albums

2010   *Teenage Dream*

2009   *Katy Perry:*
        MTV Unplugged

2008   *One of the Boys*

2001   *Katy Hudson*

Books

Baiotto, Willia. *The Katy Perry Handbook: Everything You Need to Know about Katy Perry*. LaVergne, Tennessee: Tebbo, 2010.

Tieck, Sarah. *Katy Perry: Singing Sensation*. Edina, MA: Big Buddy Books, 2011.

Works Consulted

GRAMMY.com: "2010 Nominees And Winners"
http://www.grammy.com/nominees

Greenblatt, Leah. " 'Girl' on Top: Katy Perry's Long Road—How the 'I Kissed a Girl' Songstress Finally Hit It Big." *EW.com*, July 25, 2008. http://www.ew.com/ew/article/0,,20214772,00.html

"Katy Perry Biography on LyricsReg.com"
http://www.lyricsreg.com/biography/katy+perry/

"Katy Perry Biography." *A&E Television Network*, 2011.
http://www.biography.com/articles/Katy-Perry-562678

"Katy Perry: Being a Pop Star Was My Plan." *CBS Early Show*, November 29, 2010. http://www.cbsnews.com/ stories/2010/11/29/earlyshow/leisure/main7098940.shtml

"Katy Perry: Clearing the Air on Her Faith, Her Parents and That Celibacy Vow." *Beliefnet.com*, January 29, 2009. http://blog. beliefnet.com/gospelsoundcheck/2009/01/katy-perry-clearing-the-air-on.html#ixzz16opp3fuy

"Katy Perry's 'Teenage Dream' Is No. 1." *Starpulse*, September 2, 2010. http://www.starpulse.com/news/index.php/2010/09/02/katy_ perrys_teenage_dream_is_no_1

Kinon, Cristina. "Katy Perry's Devout Christian Parents, Keith and Mary Hudson, Approve of Boyfriend Russell Brand." *New York Daily News*, December 2, 2009. http://www.nydailynews.com/ gossip/2009/12/02/2009-12-02_katy_perrys_devout_christian_ parents_keith_and_mary_hudson_approve_of_edgy_boyfr. html#ixzz16oo0h6NJ

Look to the Stars: "Katy Perry's Charity Work, Events and Causes"
http://www.looktothestars.org/celebrity/1468-katy-perry#ixzz17MzXzD6M

FURTHER READING

Lum, Linny. "Russell Brand Told Katy Perry 'Well Done' for Grammy Noms." *Hollywood News*, December 2, 2010. http://www.hollywoodnews.com/2010/12/02/russell-brand-told-katy-perry-well-done-for-grammy-noms/

Mason, Anthony. "A Play Date with Katy Perry." *CBS News*, September 26, 2010. http://www.cbsnews.com/stories/2010/09/26/sunday/main6901978.shtml

Montgomery, James. "Katy Perry 'Firework' Director Hopes Video Shows 'Substance.' " *MTV News*, October 29 2010. http://www.mtv.com/news/articles/1651128/20101029/perry_katy.jhtml

———. "Katy Perry's Evolution: Teen Church Singer to Teenage Dream." *MTV News*, May 19, 2010. http://www.mtv.com/news/articles/1639474/20100518/perry_katy.jhtml

Ngo, Ella. "Katy Perry on Russell Brand: I Found My 'Great Man of God.' " *E! Online*, November 3, 2010. http://www.eonline.com/uberblog/b209210_katy_perry_on_russell_brand_i_found_my.html

Sloame, Joanna. "*People* Magazine's 2010 Most Beautiful People List." *New York Daily News*. April 14, 2011. http://www.nydailynews.com/gossip/galleries/the_worlds_most_beautiful_people/the_worlds_most_beautiful_people.html

Stone, David. *Russell Brand and Katy Perry – The Love Story*. London, England: John Blake Publishing, Ltd., 2010.

Walls, Seth Colter. "A (Sometimes) Dirty Mind." *Newsweek*, August 25, 2010. http://www.newsweek.com/2010/08/25/teenage-dream-katy-perry-shows-her-dirty-mind.html

On the Internet

IMDb Biography for Katy Perry
   http://www.imdb.com/name/nm2953537/bio

The Official Website of Katy Perry
   http://www.katyperry.com

PHOTO CREDITS: Cover, p. 1—Jamie McCarthy/WireImage for Gigantic Perfume; p. 4—Steve Granitz/WireImage; p. 7—Frank Micelotta/PictureGroup via AP Images; p. 12—Will Ragozzino/Getty Images; p. 14—Jeffrey Mayer/WireImage; p. 16—George Napolitano/FilmMagic; p. 20—Kevin Mazur/KCA2010/WireImage; p. 22—Jon Furniss/WireImage; p. 24—Christopher Polk/Getty Images; p. 25—Graham Denholm/Getty Images; p. 26—Kevin Winter/Getty Images. Every effort has been made to locate all copyright holders of material used in this book. If any errors or omissions have occurred, corrections will be made in future editions of this book.

INDEX